TABLE OF CONTENTS

D0865604

HUMAN RIGHTS

From the very beginning of a person's life, he or she has human rights.

Human rights are privileges to which every person is automatically entitled.

All people are entitled to human rights. No person is entitled to more or less human rights than another person.

This is true regardless of the person's:

- race,
- color,
- sex,
- language,
- religion,
- opinion,
- national, ethnic, or social origin,
- property,
- disability,
- birth,
- or other status.

ASSERTING HUMAN RIGHTS

In order for human rights to be effective, people must **assert** them. This requires that people:

- **acknowledge** their human rights,

- **accept** their human rights,

- and **live** in ways that their human rights entitle them to live.

Unfortunately, many people cannot **acknowledge** their human rights because they have never been taught about their human rights and therefore do not know about them.

Many people cannot **accept** their human rights because they have been led to believe that they are not able, or do not deserve, to have human rights.

Many people cannot live in ways that their human rights entitle them to **live** because they are in situations that prevent them from having human rights.

HUMAN RIGHTS AND RESPONSIBILITY

Human rights are privileges that come with responsibility.

People who assert their human rights have a responsibility to help others assert their human rights.

This means that people who assert their human rights must help others:

- **acknowledge** their human rights,

- **accept** their human rights,

- and **live** in ways that their human rights entitle them to live.

HUMAN RIGHTS AND CHILDREN

A person younger than 18 years of age is considered to be a child.

Most children cannot completely protect and take care of themselves. They depend on adults for some of their protection and care.

Children who are dependent on adults are often deprived of their human rights.

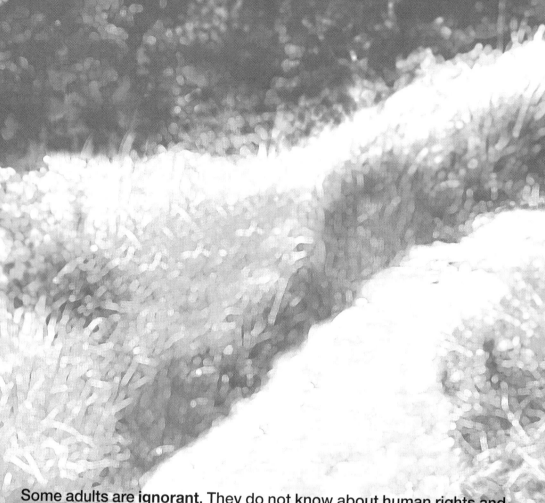

Some adults are **ignorant**. They do not know about human rights and do not teach children about them.

Some adults are **oppressed**. They have been deprived of their human rights and are not in a position from which they can help children assert their rights.

Some adults are **controlling**. They want to have complete control over children and do so by preventing children from asserting their human rights.

Some adults are **cruel**. They disregard children's human rights and do things that are harmful to children.

Adults who understand and appreciate human rights need to help protect children from adults who are:

- ignorant,

- oppressed,

- controlling,

- or cruel.

HUMAN RIGHTS ORGANIZATIONS

There are organizations that are dedicated to helping people all over the world assert their human rights. These organizations are especially dedicated to helping children assert their human rights. One of these organizations is called Amnesty International. Another organization is called the United Nations.

Amnesty International is an organization made up of individuals who go all over the world to find and expose abuses of human rights so that the abuses can be corrected.

THE CONVENTION ON THE RIGHTS OF THE CHILD

The United Nations is an organization that is made up of representatives from countries all over the world. One function of the United Nations is to advocate and support human rights worldwide.

In 1989 the United Nations put together a document called the Convention on the Rights of the Child. The document puts forth all of the Human Rights to which all children are entitled.

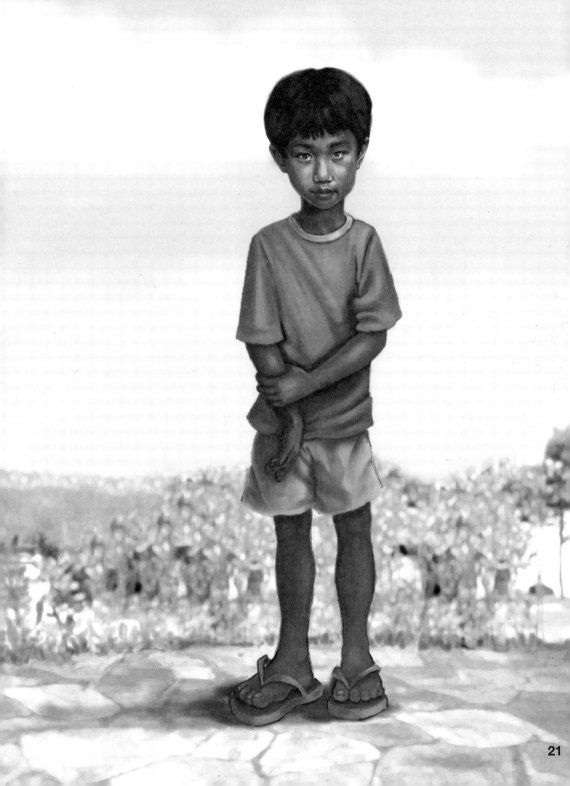

① The Right to Live
(Article 6)

Every child has the right to live.

No one has the right to threaten or take away a child's life.

Every child has the right to be protected from anyone or anything that might threaten or take away his or her life.

② The Right to Develop and Grow
(Articles 6, 29)

Every child has the right to have assistance and care that would enable the child to develop his or her:

- personality,

- talents,

- physical skills,

- mental skills,

- and social skills.

Every child has the right to develop and grow in his or her own way and at his or her own pace.

③ The Right to Have an Identity
(Articles 7, 8)

Every child has the right to have a:

- name,
- family affiliation,
- and nationality.

④ The Right to Have Parents
(Articles 3, 5, 7, 9, 10, 18, 20, 21)

Every child has the right to:

- know his or her parents,
- know where his or her parents are,
- maintain personal relationships with his or her parents,
- and have direct contact with his or her parents on a regular basis.

Every child has the right to be raised by his or her parents unless the child is taken away from them because the parents:

- neglect the child,
- or abuse the child.

When parents are unwilling or unable to protect and care for a child, the child has the right to be protected and cared for by other capable, caring adults.

(5) The Right to Have an Adequate Standard of Living
(Articles 24, 25, 26, 27, 31, 39)

Every child has the right to have a standard of living that is adequate enough for the development of the child:

- physically,

- emotionally,

- mentally,

- spiritually,

- and socially.

An adequate standard of living includes adequate:

- nutrition,

- housing,

- clothing,

- healthcare,

- education,

- recreation, and play.

6 The Right to Be Protected from All Harm
(Articles 11, 19, 20, 22, 32, 33, 34, 35, 36, 37, 38)

Every child has the right to be protected from:

- physical or mental violence,

- abuse or injury,

- neglect or negligent treatment,

- and maltreatment or exploitation.

This means that every child has the right to be protected from:

- narcotic and psychotropic drugs,

- all forms of sexual exploitation and abuse,

- abduction and the sale of the child for any purpose,

- torture, and cruel, inhuman, or degrading treatment or punishment.

The right to be protected from harm also means that no child should be forced to work at jobs before a minimum age.

Neither should the child be forced to work at jobs that might be hazardous to the child's well being or interfere with his or her education.

The right to be protected from harm also means that no child under the age of 15 should serve in armed forces.

⑦ The Right to Be Informed and Educated
(Articles 13, 17, 28, 29)

Every child has the right to seek and receive information and ideas of all kinds.

Every child has the right to have access to information and materials from a diversity of national and international sources.

A child's education should be:

- required,

- free to the child,

- based on the needs of the child,

- and based on the best interests of the child.

⑧ The Right to Have Thoughts and Beliefs
(Articles 13, 14)

Every child has the right to think his or her own thoughts and believe his or her own beliefs regarding:

- values,

- morals,

- religion,

- politics,

- and all other aspects of life.

Every child should be protected from any indoctrination that fosters racial, religious, or any other form of discrimination or hatred.

31

(9) The Right to Express Feelings and Opinions
(Articles 12, 13)

Every child has the right to express feelings and opinions:

- orally,

- in writing,

- in print,

- in the form of art,

- or through any other medium of the child's choice.

Every child has the right to have his or her feelings and opinions acknowledged and respected, especially when the feelings and opinions pertain to matters that affect the child.

(10) The Right to Have Privacy
(Article 16)

Every child has the right to keep private any information about him, or herself.

Every child has the right to keep private his or her feelings, thoughts, opinions, and communications with others.

(11) The Right to Associate with Others
(Article 15)

Every child has the right to associate and have relationships with other people.

Every child has the right to get together with groups of people as long as the gatherings are not harmful to others.

(12) The Right to Belong to a Culture or Religion
(Articles 13, 30, 31)

Every child has the right to:

- experience and enjoy his or her own culture,

- use his or her own language,

- and profess and practice his or her own religion.

(13) The Right to Be Treated Justly
(Articles 37, 39, 40)

Every child accused of breaking the law has a right to:

- be treated with dignity and respect,

- be presumed innocent until proven guilty,

- have adequate legal representation,

- and be treated fairly.

Any inflicted consequence for breaking the law should:

- take into consideration the child's age,

- be temporary,

- attempt to rehabilitate the child,

- and help the child return to society.

All 13 Children's Rights pertain to all children including children who are **disabled**:

- physically,
- emotionally,
- mentally,
- or socially.

Special care should be given to children who are disabled to insure that they are able to assert their rights.

All 13 Children's Rights pertain to all children with **special needs** who:

- have no parents,
- are unable to be raised by their parents,
- are part of extremely dysfunctional families,
- are part of families that have no resources,
- live outside of their countries,
- live in extremely deprived situations,
- or live in or around extremely dangerous situations.

Special care should also be given to children with special needs to insure that they are able to assert their rights.

CHILDREN'S RIGHTS AND YOU

If you are under 18 years of age, you are considered to be a child. If you are a child, you are automatically entitled to these rights:

(1) The Right to Live

(2) The Right to Develop and Grow

(3) The Right to Have an Identity

(4) The Right to Have Parents

(5) The Right to Have an Adequate Standard of Living

(6) The Right to Be Protected from All Harm

(7) The Right to Be Informed and Educated

(8) The Right to Have Thoughts and Beliefs

(9) The Right to Express Feelings and Opinions

(10) The Right to Have Privacy

(11) The Right to Associate with Others

(12) The Right to Belong to a Culture or Religion

(13) The Right to Be Treated Justly

In order for your rights to be effective, you must **assert** them. This requires that you:

- **acknowledge** your rights,

- **accept** your rights,

- and **live** in ways that your rights entitle you to live.

If you are having difficulty asserting any of your rights, you need to get someone to help you correct your situation.

Choose a person you trust. Make sure that it is someone who is old enough and wise enough to help you. It might be a:

- parent,

- guardian,

- teacher,

- principal,

- school counselor,

- religious leader,

- close relative (such as a grandparent, aunt, or uncle),

- or an adult friend.

If the adult you talk to does not help you, talk to other adults. Keep talking to people until you find someone to help you.

Children's rights come with responsibility.

If you assert your rights, you have a responsibility to encourage and support other children to assert their rights.

This means that you must encourage and support other children to:

- **acknowledge** their rights,

- **accept** their rights,

- and **live** in ways that their rights entitle them to live.

Also, if you think that a child is being deprived of his or her rights, you need to encourage him or her to talk to a caring adult.

You might also want to talk to an adult about the situation to make sure that the child gets help.

If the adult you talk to does not help to correct the situation, talk to other adults. Keep talking to people until you find someone who can help.

Unfortunately, millions of children all over the world are not allowed to assert their rights.

Amnesty International and other human rights organizations work to help these children assert their rights.

You can help children who are being deprived of their rights by supporting the work of Amnesty International and other organizations that are concerned about human rights.

Children's Rights are special rights that pertain to you and every other child in the world.

Children's Rights help make it possible for you to survive and grow so that you can be the wonderful person you are meant to be.

MINE AND YOURS
Human Rights for Kids

Published in the United States by powerHouse kids
a division of powerHouse Cultural Entertainment, Inc.
68 Charlton Street, New York, NY 10014-4601
telephone 212 604 9074, fax 212 366 5247
e-mail: info@powerhousekids.net
website: www.powerHousekids.net

First edition, 2005

Library of Congress Cataloging-in-Publication Data:

Berry, Joy.
    Mine & yours : human rights for kids / by Joy Berry ; illustrations by Nicole Richardson ; in association with Amnesty International.-- 1st ed.
      p. cm.
    ISBN 1-57687-260-2 (pbk.)
    1. Children's rights--Juvenile literature. I. Title: Mine and yours. II. Richardson, Nicole, ill. III. Amnesty International. IV. Title.

    HQ789.B48 2005
    323.3'52--dc22

                                                                 2005047264

Paperback ISBN 1-57687-260-2

Separations, printing, and binding by Pimlico Book International, Hong Kong

A complete catalog of powerHouse kids is available upon request; please call, write, or visit our website.

For more information about Amnesty International, visit www.amnestyusa.org or call 1-800-AMNESTY.

10 9 8 7 6 5 4 3 2 1

Printed and bound in China